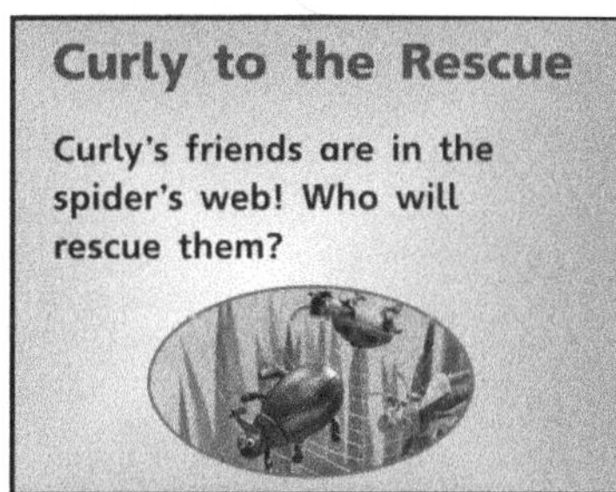

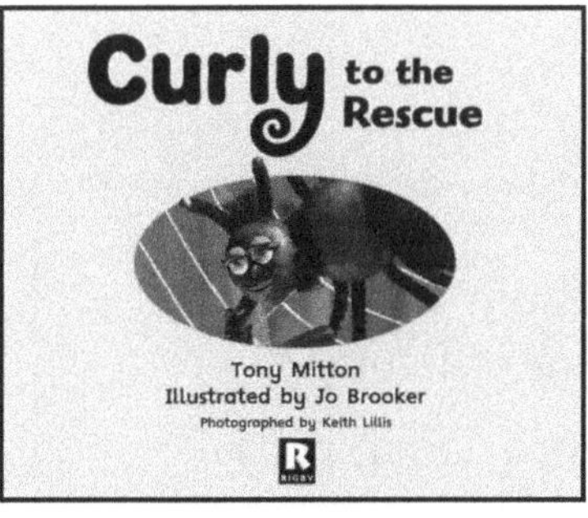

Walkthrough

This is a story about Curly.

Can you remember the other Curly stories you have read?

Let's read the title: 'Curly to the Rescue'.

Who else is in the picture?

Do you think Spider is a nice character?

Walkthrough

Let's read the blurb together.

What will the spider do to Curly's friends?

Walkthrough

Let's read the title together: 'Curly to the Rescue'.

Which character can we see in this picture?

What do spiders like to eat? How do they catch their food?

Jo Brooker made the plasticine models and Keith Lillis took the photographs of them.

Walkthrough

What is the spider saying to the ladybird?

What do you think she is trying to do?

What will happen if the ladybird goes up to see the spider?

 **Observe and Prompt**

Word Recognition

- Check the children can read 'little'. Help them with the 'le' sound at the end of the word if they have difficulty.

- If the children have difficulty with the word 'ladybird', ask them to break it down into three syllables, before blending the whole word together (left to right).

- Check the children can read the word 'spider' using their decoding skills. Check they can read the adjacent consonants 'sp' at the beginning of the word.

Observe and Prompt

Language Comprehension

- Ask the children what the spider says to the ladybird.
- What do the children think the spider is trying to do?
- Do the children think she is being friendly to the ladybird?

Walkthrough

Who has come along? What colour is
the grasshopper? (*green*)

Will the spider want to catch him in her web?

What will she call out to him?

 **Observe and Prompt**

Word Recognition

- Check the children can read the sight words 'come', 'said' and 'the'.

- Check the children can read 'green' using their decoding skills. Check they can read the adjacent consonants 'gr' at the beginning of the word.

- If the children have difficulty with the word 'grasshopper', ask them to break it down into three syllables – 'grass', 'hop' and 'per', before blending the whole word together (left to right).

4

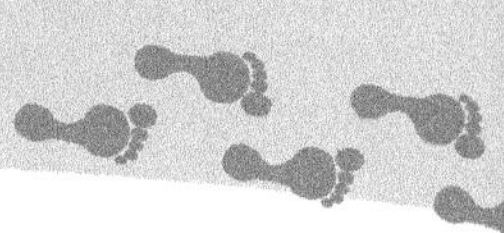

Observe and Prompt

Language Comprehension

- Observe reading with expression.
- Ask the children what the spider says to the grasshopper.
- Why do the children think she wants the grasshopper to come up and see her?
- Ask the children who else they think will come along.

Walkthrough

What kind of creature is this? Is it little or big?

What will the spider say?

Who is trapped in the spider's web now?

What will happen to them?

 **Observe and Prompt**

Word Recognition

- Check the children are using their decoding skills to read the CVC word 'big'.

- Check the children can read the word 'beetle' using their decoding skills. Help them with the 'le' sound at the end of this word if you have not yet taught this.

- Check the children can read 'see' and 'me'.

6

Observe and Prompt

Language Comprehension

- Explain the pattern of the text so far (alliterative phrases) and ask what other word could have been used to describe the beetle. (*blue*)

- What do the children think the spider is trying to do?

- What do the children think will happen next?

The spider smiled.
"Hee hee!" she said.
"Now I will eat the ladybird
and the grasshopper and
the beetle for my tea."

8

 **Observe and Prompt**

Word Recognition

- Check the children can read 'smiled' using their decoding skills. If the children have difficulty, model the reading of this word for them.

- Check the children can read 'Now', helping them with the 'ow' sound if they have difficulty.

- Check the children can read the words 'eat' and 'tea' using their decoding skills. Help them with the 'ea' sound if they struggle. Explain that these words have the same 'ee' vowel sound as 'Hee hee' and 'beetle' but are spelled differently.

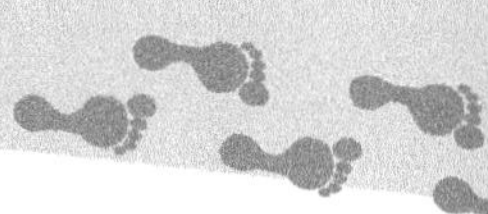

Observe and Prompt

Language Comprehension

- Prompt for expressive reading.

- Ask the children what the spider says.

- How do the children think the spider feels? How do they think the other creatures feel?

- What do the children think will happen next? Will the spider eat the creatures?

Who came along? Where might the spider
have gone?

What are the other creatures calling out to him?

What do you think Curly is thinking?

 **Observe and Prompt**

Word Recognition

- Check the children can read 'Along' and 'Curly' using their decoding skills.

- Check the children can read 'Help' using their decoding skills.

- Check the children can read 'going' using their decoding skills. Help them with the 'ing' suffix at the end of the word.

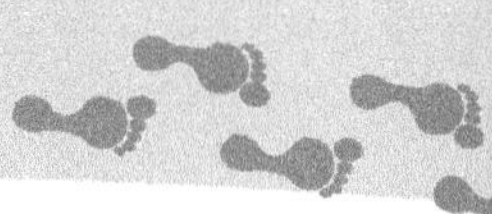

Observe and Prompt

Language Comprehension

- Observe reading with expression for the words in bold.
- Ask the children who came along.
- Ask the children what the creatures call out to Curly.
- Do the children think Curly will be able to rescue them?

Walkthrough

Curly goes to look for help. Who does he see?

What might Curly tell the Snail?

What do you think they will do?

Curly saw the snail.
"Help!" he said.
"The spider is going to eat
the ladybird and the
grasshopper and the beetle!"

12

 **Observe and Prompt**

Word Recognition

- Check the children can read 'snail' using their decoding skills. Can they read the adjacent consonants 'sn' at the start of the word? Help them with the 'ai' sound if they struggle with this word.

- Check the children can read the sight words 'saw', 'and' and 'the'.

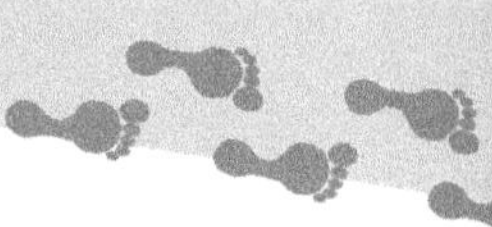

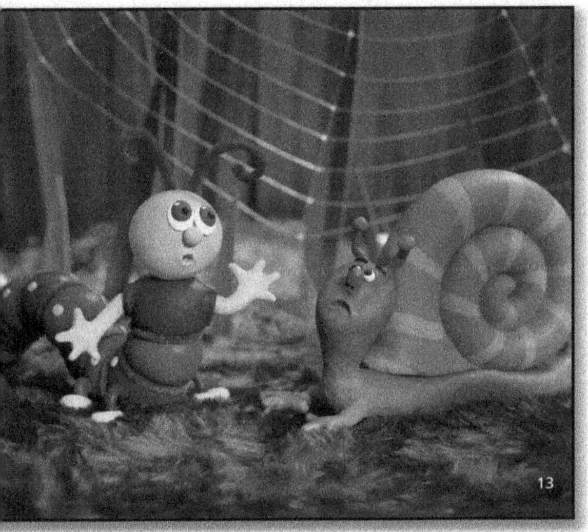

Observe and Prompt

Language Comprehension

- Check the children have noticed the speech marks and are reading with expression.

- Ask the children what Curly says to the snail.

- How do the children think Curly and the snail will help the other creatures?

Walkthrough

What did Curly and the snail do to the web?

Did the plan work?

What will happen next?

Observe and Prompt

Word Recognition

- Check the children can read 'pulled', having noticed the 'ed' suffix.

- Check the children can read the CVC word 'web' using their decoding skills.

- Check the children can read 'Down' using their decoding skills. Help them with the 'ow' sound if they have difficulty.

 ## Observe and Prompt

Language Comprehension

- Ask the children what Curly and the snail did.
- Check the children understand what happened to the web.
- Do the children think the creatures will be safe now?
- What do the children think the creatures will say?

Walkthrough

What do you think the creatures said when Curly set them free?

What did they do after they got free from the web?

What would you have done?

Observe and Prompt

Word Recognition

- Check the children can read 'Hurray' and 'away' using their decoding skills.

- Check the children can read the CVC word 'ran' using their decoding skills.

Language Comprehension

- Prompt for expressive reading

- Ask the children what the creatures say.

- How do the children think they all feel?